Saint Joseph

Missal Guide

2014

Jan. 1 to Dec. 31, 2014

A handy calendar indicating the Mass and texts that may be said on each day

for the

ST. JOSEPH SUNDAY MISSAL (T-820) (© 2011)

(indicated in boldface)

and the

ST. JOSEPH WEEKDAY MISSAL (T-920-921)

(© 2011, 2012)

(indicated in lightface)

No. 920/G

CATHOLIC BOOK PUBLISHING CORP.
New Jersey
www.catholicbookpublishing.com

LIST OF ABBREVIATIONS

A — Antiphons
Ab — Abbot
ALL — All parts of the Mass
AP — see p. 3
B — Bishop (Bb — Bishops)
BVM — Blessed Virgin Mary
Comp(s) — Companion(s)
D — Doctor of the Church
(Dd — Doctors of the Church)
F — Feast
G — Gospel
II — Year II
M — Martyr (Mm — Martyrs)
Mem — Memorial (Obligatory)
Opt. — Optional
Or. — Oration
P with no.,
e.g., P 11 — Preface number
Pr — Priest (Pp — Priests)
Pref. — Preface
RC — see p. 3
RI — Reading I
RII — Reading II
Rel — Religious
Sol — Solemnity
V — Virgin (Vv — Virgins)
* — see p. 3

No. 920/G

Printed in the U.S.A.

www.catholicbookpublishing.com

INTRODUCTION

The St. Joseph Missals give full instructions for each Mass. Since different cycles of Readings are used from year to year, this Guide lists the Mass or Masses for each day and refers to the page or pages on which they may be found in the Missals. This Guide is keyed to the latest editions of the Missals; i.e., *New St. Joseph Sunday Missal, Complete Edition,* © 2011 and *New Saint Joseph Weekday Missal, Complete Edition* (2 Vols.), © 2011, 2012. Follow the Mass as given in the Missals except where special directions or differences are noted in the Guide. Keep in mind the many options available to the Celebrant as is explained under the asterisk (*) below. (This year the readings are those of Year A for Sunday and Year II for Weekdays. Advent 2014, Year B.)

Antiphons and Prayers (Entrance Antiphon, Communion Antiphon, Collect, Prayer over the Offerings, and Prayer after Communion) are abbreviated as AP.

Readings and Intervenient Chants (Reading I, Responsorial Psalm, Reading II, Alleluia or Gospel Verse, and Gospel) are abbreviated as RC.

The *Gloria* and *Creed (Profession of Faith)* are said only when they are so specified in the Calendar.

Prefaces in the Masses of Saints with the rank of Memorials may be taken from the Commons or from the Liturgical Time, although only the latter is mentioned in the Guide.

* On Weekdays in Ordinary Time, many options are permissible as is explained in 4e on page [13] in the St. Joseph Weekday Missal. See Vol. II, pages 1-2, 427-429 and 1041 for more detailed information. In accord with what is said on pages 427-429, the Guide refers solely to the *preferred* weekday readings and, where they occur, the *special* or *proper* readings for Saints. No mention is made of the *appropriate* readings given or listed on each Saint day or the *general* readings found in the Commons which also may be said, but only under certain conditions as indicated on pages 427-428.

VOLUME I
January 1 to June 8, 2014

JANUARY

1. **Wed. OCTAVE DAY OF THE NATIVITY OF THE LORD [CHRISTMAS]; SOLEMNITY OF MARY, THE HOLY MOTHER OF GOD (Sol) (Holyday of Obligation)**
ALL **168**; Gloria, Creed; Pref. P 56, p. **172**

2. Thu. Sts. Basil the Great & Gregory Nazianzen, B & D (Mem) (961)
AP 961; RC 122-123; Pref. P 3-5, pp. 700-701

OR: Mass of Our Lord Jesus Christ, the Eternal High Priest (1st Thu.)
AP 1348-1349; RC 122-123; Pref. P 47-48, pp. 711-712

3. Fri. Christmas Weekday
AP 119-120; RC 124-125; Pref. P 3-5, pp. 700-701

OR: The Most Holy Name of Jesus (962)
AP 962-963; RC 124-125; Pref. P 3-5, pp. 700-701

OR: Mass of the Most Sacred Heart of Jesus (1st Fri.)
AP 1352-1354; RC 124-125; Pref. P 45, p. 1353

4. Sat. St. Elizabeth Ann Seton, Rel (Mem) (964)
AP 964-965; RC 125-127; Pref. P 3-5, pp. 700-701

OR: Mass of the Immaculate Heart of the BVM (1st Sat.)
AP 1069-1071; RC 125-127; Pref. P 56-57, pp. 715-716

EVENING: **VIGIL MASS OF THE EPIPHANY OF THE LORD (Sol)** Sunday Missal
ALL **179**; Gloria, Creed; Pref. P 6, p. **184**

5. **Sun. THE EPIPHANY OF THE LORD (Sol)**
ALL **186**; Gloria, Creed; Pref. P 6, p. **184**

6. Mon. Monday after the Solemnity of the Epiphany
ALL 135-138; Pref. P 6, p. 701

OR: St. André Bessette, Rel (967)
AP 1164-1166; RC 135; Pref. P 6, p. 701

7. Tue. Tuesday after the Solemnity of the Epiphany
   ALL 139-141; Pref. P 6, p. 701

OR: St. Raymond of Penyafort, Pr (967)
   AP 1133-1135; RC 139; Pref. P 6, p. 701

8. Wed. Wednesday after the Solemnity of the Epiphany
   ALL 142-145; Pref. P 6, p. 701

9. Thu. Thursday after the Solemnity of the Epiphany
   ALL 145-148; Pref. P 6, p. 701

10. Fri. Friday after the Solemnity of the Epiphany
   ALL 148-150; Pref. P 6, p. 701

11. Sat. Saturday after the Solemnity of the Epiphany
   ALL 151-153; Pref. P 6, p. 701

12. **Sun. BAPTISM OF THE LORD (F)**
   ALL **188**; Gloria, Creed; Pref. P 7, p. **193**

13. Mon. Monday of the 1st Week in Ordinary Time*
   AP 156 (1st Week) or (1st-34th Week) 156-202
   RC 206 (II); Pref. P 37-42, pp. 708-710

OR: St. Hilary, B & D (968)
   AP 1128-1131 or 1144-1146; RC 206 (II); Pref. P 37-42, pp. 708-710

14. Tue. Tuesday of the 1st Week in Ordinary Time*
   AP 156 (1st Week) or (1st-34th Week) 156-202
   RC 210 (II); Pref. P 37-42, pp. 708-710

15. Wed. Wednesday of the 1st Week in Ordinary Time*
   AP 156 (1st Week) or (1st-34th Week) 156-202
   RC 214 (II); Pref. P 37-42, pp. 708-710

16. Thu. Thursday of the 1st Week in Ordinary Time*
   AP 156 (1st Week) or (1st-34th Week) 156-202
   RC 217 (II); Pref. P 37-42, pp. 708-710

17. Fri. St. Anthony, Ab (Mem) (969)
   AP 970; RC 221 (II); Pref. P 37-42, pp. 708-710

18. Sat. Saturday of the 1st Week in Ordinary Time*
AP 156 (1st Week) or (1st-34th Week) 156-202
RC 225 (II); Pref. P 37-42, pp. 708-710

OR: Mass of the BVM on Saturday
AP 1090-1099; RC 225 (II); Pref. P 56-57, pp. 715-176

19. **Sun. SECOND SUNDAY IN ORDINARY TIME**
ALL **195**; Gloria, Creed; Pref. P 29-36, pp. **88-92**

20. Mon. Monday of the 2nd Week in Ordinary Time*
AP 157 (2nd Week) or (1st-34th Week) 156-202
RC 229 (II); Pref. P 37-42, pp. 708-710

OR: St. Fabian, Po & M (972)
AP 1112-1115 or 1125-1128; RC 229 (II); Pref. P 37-42, pp. 708-710

OR: St. Sebastian, M (972)
AP 1112-1115; RC 229 (II); Pref. P 37-42, pp. 708-710

21. Tue. St. Agnes, V & M (Mem) (973)
AP 1122-1123 or 1148-1151; RC 232 (II)
Pref. P 37-42, pp. 708-710

22. Wed. Day of Prayer for the Legal Protection of Unborn Children (974)
AP 1345-1347 or 1335-1336; RC 236 (II)
Pref. P 37-42, pp. 708-710

23. Thu. Thursday of the 2nd Week in Ordinary Time*
AP 157 (2nd Week) or (1st-34th Week) 156-202
RC 240 (II); Pref. P 37-42, pp. 708-710

OR: St. Vincent, Deacon & M (974)
AP 1112-1115; RC 240 (II); Pref. P 37-42, pp. 708-710

24. Fri. St. Francis de Sales, B & D (Mem) (975)
AP 1128-1131 or 1144-1146; RC 245 (II);
Pref. P 37-42, pp. 708-710

25. Sat. THE CONVERSION OF ST. PAUL, APOSTLE (F)
ALL 976, Gloria; Pref. P 64, pp. 716-717

26. **Sun. THIRD SUNDAY IN ORDINARY TIME**
ALL **200**; Gloria, Creed; Pref. P 29-36, pp. **88-92**

27. Mon. Monday of the 3rd Week in Ordinary Time*
AP 158 (3rd Week) or (1st-34th Week) 156-202
RC 252 (II); Pref. P 37-42, pp. 708-710

OR: St. Angela Merici, V (984)
AP 1148-1152 or 1168-1170; RC 252 (II); Pref. P 37-42, pp. 708-710

28. Tue. St. Thomas Aquinas, Pr & D (Mem) (985)
AP 1144-1146 or 1133-1135; RC 256 (II);
Pref. P 37-42, pp. 708-710

29. Wed. Wednesday of the 3rd Week in Ordinary Time*
AP 158 (3rd Week) or (1st-34th Week) 156-202
RC 259 (II); Pref. P 37-42, pp. 708-710

30. Thu. Thursday of the 3rd Week in Ordinary Time*
AP 158 (3rd Week) or (1st-34th Week) 156-202
RC 263 (II); Pref. P 37-42, pp. 708-710

31. Fri. St. John Bosco, Pr (Mem) (985)
AP 1133-1135 or 1168-1169; RC 267 (II);
Pref. P 37-42, pp. 708-710

FEBRUARY

1. Sat. Saturday of the 3rd Week in Ordinary Time*
AP 158 (3rd Week) or (1st-34th Week) 156-202
RC 271 (II); Pref. P 37-42, pp. 708-710

OR: Mass of the Immaculate Heart of the BVM (1st Sat.)
AP 1069-1071; RC 271 (II); Pref. P 56-57, pp. 715-716

OR: Mass of the BVM on Saturday
AP 1090-1099; RC 271 (II); Pref. P 56-57, pp. 715-716

2. **Sun. THE PRESENTATION OF THE LORD (F)**
ALL **1402**; Gloria, Creed; Pref. P 49, p. **1407**

3. Mon. Monday of the 4th Week in Ordinary Time*
AP 160 (4th Week) or (1st-34th Week) 156-202
RC 276 (II); Pref. P 37-42, pp. 708-710

OR: St. Blaise, B & M (995)
AP 1112-1115 or 1128-1131; RC 276 (II); Pref. P 37-42, pp. 708-710

OR: St. Ansgar, B (996)
AP 1138-1143 or 1128-1131; RC 276 (II); Pref. P 37-42, pp. 708-710

4. Tue. Tuesday of the 4th Week in Ordinary Time*
AP 160 (4th Week) or (1st-34th Week) 156-202
RC 280 (II); Pref. P 37-42, pp. 708-710

5. Wed. St. Agatha, V & M (Mem) (996)
AP 1122-1123 or 1148-1152; RC 285 (II)
Pref. P 37-42, pp. 708-710

6. Thu. St. Paul Miki & Comps, Mm (Mem) (997)
AP 1104-1112; RC 289 (II); Pref. P 37-42, pp. 708-710

OR: Mass of Our Lord Jesus Christ, the Eternal High Priest (1st Thu.)
AP 1348-1349; RC 289 (II); Pref. P 47-48, pp. 711-712

7. Fri. Friday of the 4th Week in Ordinary Time*
AP 160 (4th Week) or (1st-34th Week) 156-202
RC 292 (II); Pref. P 37-42, pp. 708-710

OR: Mass of the Most Sacred Heart of Jesus (1st Fri.)
AP 1352-1354; RC 292 (II); Pref. P 45, p. 1353

8. Sat. Saturday of the 4th Week in Ordinary Time*
AP 160 (4th Week) or (1st-34th Week) 156-202
RC 296 (II); Pref. P 37-42, pp. 708-710

OR: St. Jerome Emiliani (998)
AP 1168-1169; RC 296 (II); Pref. P 37-42, pp. 708-710

OR: St. Josephine Bakhita, V (998)
AP 1148-1152; RC 296 (II); Pref. P 37-42, pp. 708-710

OR: Mass of the BVM on Saturday
AP 1090-1099; RC 296 (II); Pref. P 56-57, pp. 715-716

9. **Sun. FIFTH SUNDAY IN ORDINARY TIME**
ALL **212**; Gloria, Creed; Pref. P 29-36, pp. **88-92**

10. Mon. St. Scholastica, V (Mem) (999)
AP 1148-1152 or 1163-1164; RC 304 (II);
Pref. P 37-42, pp. 708-710

11. Tue. Tuesday of the 5th Week in Ordinary Time*
AP 161 (5th Week) or (1st-34th Week) 156-202
RC 308 (II); Pref. P 37-42, pp. 708-710

OR: Our Lady of Lourdes (1000)
AP 1090-1099; RC 308 (II); Pref. P 56-57, pp. 715-716

12. Wed. Wednesday of the 5th Week in Ordinary Time*
AP 161 (5th Week) or (1st-34th Week) 156-202
RC 311 (II); Pref. P 37-42, pp. 708-710

13. Thu. Thursday of the 5th Week in Ordinary Time*
AP 161 (5th Week) or (1st-34th Week) 156-202
RC 315 (II); Pref. P 37-42, pp. 708-710

14. Fri. Sts. Cyril, Monk, & Methodius, B (Mem) (1001)
AP 1001-1002; RC 319 (II);
Pref. P 37-42, pp. 708-710

15. Sat. Saturday of the 5th Week in Ordinary Time*
AP 161 (5th Week) or (1st-34th Week) 156-202
RC 323 (II); Pref. P 37-42, pp. 708-710

OR: Mass of the BVM on Saturday
AP 1090-1099; RC 323 (II); Pref. P 56-57, pp. 715-716

16. **Sun. SIXTH SUNDAY IN ORDINARY TIME**
ALL **217**; Gloria, Creed; Pref. P 29-36, pp. **88-92**

17. Mon. Monday of the 6th Week in Ordinary Time*
AP 162 (6th Week) or (1st-34th Week) 156-202
RC 327 (II); Pref. P 37-42, pp. 708-710

OR: The Seven Holy Founders of the Servite Order (1003)
AP 1164-1166; RC 327 (II); Pref. P 37-42, pp. 708-710

18. Tue. Tuesday of the 6th Week in Ordinary Time*
AP 162 (6th Week) or (1st-34th Week) 156-202
RC 330 (II); Pref. P 37-42, pp. 708-710

19. Wed. Wednesday of the 6th Week in Ordinary Time*
AP 162 (6th Week) or (1st-34th Week) 156-202
RC 334 (II); Pref. P 37-42, pp. 708-710

20. Thu. Thursday of the 6th Week in Ordinary Time*
AP 162 (6th Week) or (1st-34th Week) 156-202
RC 338 (II); Pref. P 37-42, pp. 708-710

21. Fri. Friday of the 6th Week in Ordinary Time*
AP 162 (6th Week) or (1st-34th Week) 156-202
RC 342 (II); Pref. P 37-42, pp. 708-710

OR: St. Peter Damian, B & D (1003)
AP 1144-1146 or 1128-1131; RC 342 (II); Pref. P 37-42, pp. 708-710

22. Sat. THE CHAIR OF ST. PETER, APOSTLE (F)
ALL 1004; Gloria, Pref. P 64, p. 716

23. **Sun. SEVENTH SUNDAY IN ORDINARY TIME**
ALL **224**; Gloria, Creed; Pref. P 29-36, pp. **88-92**

24. Mon. Monday of the 7th Week in Ordinary Time*
AP 164 (7th Week) or (1st-34th Week) 156-202
RC 350 (II); Pref. P 37-42, pp. 708-710

25. Tue. Tuesday of the 7th Week in Ordinary Time*
AP 164 (7th Week) or (1st-34th Week) 156-202
RC 354 (II); Pref. P 37-42, pp. 708-710

26. Wed. Wednesday of the 7th Week in Ordinary Time*
AP 164 (7th Week) or (1st-34th Week) 156-202
RC 358 (II); Pref. P 37-42, pp. 708-710

27. Thu. Thursday of the 7th Week in Ordinary Time*
AP 164 (7th Week) or (1st-34th Week) 156-202
RC 361 (II); Pref. P 37-42, pp. 708-710

28. Fri. Friday of the 7th Week in Ordinary Time*
AP 164 (7th Week) or (1st-34th Week) 156-202
RC 364 (II); Pref. P 37-42, pp. 708-710

MARCH

1. Sat. Saturday of the 7th Week in Ordinary Time*
AP 164 (7th Week) or (1st-34th Week) 156-202
RC 368 (II); Pref. P 37-42, pp. 708-710

OR: Mass of the Immaculate Heart of the BVM (1st Sat.)
AP 1069; RC 271 (II); Pref. P 56-57, pp. 715-716

OR: Mass of the BVM on Saturday
AP 1090-1099; RC 368 (II); Pref. P 56-57, pp. 715-716

2. **Sun. EIGHTH SUNDAY IN ORDINARY TIME**
ALL **229**; Gloria, Creed; Pref. P 29-36, pp. **88-92**

3. Mon. Monday of the 8th Week in Ordinary Time*
AP 165 (8th Week) or (1st-34th Week) 156-202
RC 371 (II); Pref. P 37-42, pp. 708-710

OR: St. Katharine Drexel, V (1009)
AP 1148-1152; RC 371 (II); Pref. P 37-42, pp. 708-710

4. Tue. Tuesday of the 8th Week in Ordinary Time*
AP 165 (8th Week) or (1st-34th Week) 156-202
RC 375 (II); Pref. P 37-42, pp. 708-710

OR: St. Casimir (1009)
AP 1158-1160; RC 375 (II); Pref. P 37-42, pp. 708-710

5. Wed. ASH WEDNESDAY
ALL 421 (**243**); Pref. P 10-11, p. 703

6. Thu. Thursday after Ash Wednesday
ALL 428; Pref. P 8-11, pp. 702-703

7. Fri. Friday after Ash Wednesday
ALL 431 (Opt. Or. of Sts. Perpetua & Felicity, Mm, p. 1010)
Pref. P 8-11, pp. 702-703

8. Sat. Saturday after Ash Wednesday
ALL 435 (Opt. Or. of St. John of God, Rel, p. 1011)
Pref. P 8-11, pp. 702-703

9. **Sun. FIRST SUNDAY OF LENT**
ALL **251**; Creed

10. Mon. Monday of the 1st Week of Lent
ALL 438: Pref. P 8-11, pp. 702-703
11. Tue. Tuesday of the 1st Week of Lent
ALL 442; Pref. P 8-11, pp. 702-703
12. Wed. Wednesday of the 1st Week of Lent
ALL 445; Pref. P 8-11, pp. 702-703
13. Thu. Thursday of the 1st Week of Lent
ALL 449; Pref. P 8-11, pp. 702-703
14. Fri. Friday of the 1st Week of Lent
ALL 452; Pref. P 8-11, pp. 702-703
15. Sat. Saturday of the 1st Week of Lent
ALL 456; Pref. P 8-11, pp. 702-703
16. **Sun. SECOND SUNDAY OF LENT**
ALL **259**; Creed
17. Mon. Monday of the 2nd Week of Lent
ALL 459 (Opt. Or. of St. Patrick, B, p. 1013)
Pref. P 8-11, pp. 702-703
18. Tue. Tuesday of the 2nd Week of Lent
ALL 462 (Opt. Or. of St. Cyril of Jerusalem, B & D, p. 1013)
Pref. P 8-11, pp. 702-703
19. Wed. ST. JOSEPH, SPOUSE OF THE BVM (Sol)
ALL 1014; Gloria, Creed
20. Thu. Thursday of the 2nd Week of Lent
ALL 469; Pref. P 8-11, pp. 702-703
21. Fri. Friday of the 2nd Week of Lent
ALL 473; Pref. P 8-11, pp. 702-703
22. Sat. Saturday of the 2nd Week of Lent
ALL 478; Pref. P 8-11, pp. 702-703
23. **Sun. THIRD SUNDAY OF LENT**
ALL **265**; Creed; Pref. P 8-9, pp. **84-85** or P 14, p. **272**
24. Mon. Monday of the 3rd Week of Lent
ALL 486; Pref. P 8-11, pp. 702-703

25. Tue. THE ANNUNCIATION OF THE LORD (Sol)
ALL 1020; Gloria, Creed

26. Wed. Wednesday of the 3rd Week of Lent
ALL 494; Pref. P 8-11, pp. 702-703

27. Thu. Thursday of the 3rd Week of Lent
ALL 497; Pref. P 8-11, pp. 702-703

28. Fri. Friday of the 3rd Week of Lent
ALL 501; Pref. P 8-11, pp. 702-703

29. Sat. Saturday of the 3rd Week of Lent
ALL 505; Pref. P 8-11, pp. 702-703

30. **Sun. FOURTH SUNDAY OF LENT**
ALL **275**; Creed; Pref. P 8-9, pp. **84-85** or P 15, p. **283**

31. Mon. Monday of the 4th Week of Lent
ALL 512; Pref. P 8-11, pp. 702-703

APRIL

1. Tue. Tuesday of the 4th Week of Lent
ALL 515; Pref. P 8-11, pp. 702-703

2. Wed. Wednesday of the 4th Week of Lent
ALL 520 (Opt. Or. of St. Francis of Paola, Hermit, p. 1025)
Pref. P 8-11, pp. 702-703

3. Thu. Thursday of the 4th Week of Lent
ALL 524; Pref. P 8-11, pp. 702-703

4. Fri. Friday of the 4th Week of Lent
ALL 528 (Opt. Or. of St. Isidore, B & D, p. 1025)
Pref. P 8-11, pp. 702-703

5. Sat. Saturday of the 4th Week of Lent
ALL 532 (Opt. Or. of St. Vincent Ferrer, Pr, p. 1026)
Pref. P 8-11, pp. 702-703

6. **Sun. FIFTH SUNDAY OF LENT**
ALL **286**; Creed; Pref. P 8-9, pp. **84-85** or P 16, p. **293**

7. Mon. Monday of the 5th Week of Lent
ALL 539 (Opt. Or. of St. John Baptist de la Salle, Pr, p. 1027)
Pref. P 17, pp. 703-704

8. Tue. Tuesday of the 5th Week of Lent
ALL 547; Pref. P 17, pp. 703-704

9. Wed. Wednesday of the 5th Week of Lent
ALL 550; Pref. P 17, pp. 703-704

10. Thu. Thursday of the 5th Week of Lent
ALL 555; Pref. P 17, pp. 703-704

11. Fri. Friday of the 5th Week of Lent
ALL 558 (Opt. Or. of St. Stanislaus, B & M, p. 1028)
Pref. P 17, pp. 703-704

12. Sat. Saturday of the 5th Week of Lent
ALL 562; Pref. P 17, pp. 703-704

13. **Sun. PALM SUNDAY OF THE PASSION OF THE LORD**
ALL **296**; Mass **305**; Creed; Pref. P 19, p. **318**

14. Mon. MONDAY OF HOLY WEEK
ALL 567; Pref. P 18, p. 704

15. Tue. TUESDAY OF HOLY WEEK
ALL 571; Pref. P 18, p. 704

16. Wed. WEDNESDAY OF HOLY WEEK
ALL 575; Pref. P 18, p. 704

17. Thu. THURSDAY OF HOLY WEEK [HOLY THURSDAY]
Chrism Mass: ALL 579 **(320)**; Gloria
Mass of the Lord's Supper: ALL 586 **(328)**;
Gloria; Pref. P 47, p. 711 **(92)**

18. Fri. FRIDAY OF THE PASSION OF THE LORD [GOOD FRIDAY]
ALL 597 **(342)**

19. Sat. HOLY SATURDAY (Weekday Missal)
EASTER VIGIL IN THE HOLY NIGHT; ALL 745 **(373)**; Gloria;
(Year A) **408** (777); Pref. P 21, p. **85** (704)

20. **Sun. EASTER SUNDAY**
ALL **424**; Gloria; Creed; Pref. P 21, p. **85**

21. Mon. MONDAY WITHIN THE OCTAVE OF EASTER
ALL 793; Gloria; Pref. P 21, p. 704

22. Tue. TUESDAY WITHIN THE OCTAVE OF EASTER
ALL 797; Gloria; Pref. P 21, p. 704

23. Wed. WEDNESDAY WITHIN THE OCTAVE OF EASTER
ALL 801; Gloria; Pref. P 21, p. 704

24. Thu. THURSDAY WITHIN THE OCTAVE OF EASTER
ALL 805; Gloria; Pref. P 21, p. 704

25. Fri. FRIDAY WITHIN THE OCTAVE OF EASTER
ALL 809; Gloria; Pref. P 21, p. 704

26. Sat. SATURDAY WITHIN THE OCTAVE OF EASTER
ALL 813; Gloria, Pref. P 21, p. 704

27. **Sun. SECOND SUNDAY OF EASTER (OR OF DIVINE MERCY)**
ALL **434**; Gloria; Creed; Pref. P 21, p. **85**

28. Mon. Monday of the 2nd Week of Easter
ALL 817; Pref. P 21-25, pp. 704-706

OR: St. Peter Chanel, Pr & M (1035)
AP 1118-1119 or 1138-1143; RC 818
Pref. P 21-25, pp. 704-706

OR: St. Louis Grignion de Montfort, Pr (1036)
AP 1133-1135; RC 818
Pref. P 21-25, pp. 704-706

29. Tue. St. Catherine of Siena, V & D (Mem) (1037)
AP 1037; RC 821; Pref. P 21-25, pp. 704-706

30. Wed. Wednesday of the 2nd Week of Easter
ALL 824; Pref. P 21-25, pp. 704-706

OR: St. Pius V, Po (1039)
AP 1125-1128, RC 824
Pref. P 21-25, pp. 704-706

MAY

1. Thu. Thursday of the 2nd Week of Easter
ALL 827; Pref. P 21-25, pp. 704-706

OR: St. Joseph the Worker (1040)
ALL 1040

OR: Mass of Our Lord Jesus Christ, the Eternal High Priest (1st Thu.)
AP 1348-1349; RC 828; Pref. P 47-48, pp. 711-712

2. Fri. St. Athanasius, B & D (Mem) (1044)
AP 1045-1046; RC 831 (G 1045); Pref. P 21-25, pp. 704-706

OR: Mass of the Most Sacred Heart of Jesus (1st Fri.)
AP 1352-1354; RC 831; Pref. P 45, p. 1353

3. Sat. STS. PHILIP & JAMES, APOSTLES (F)
ALL 1046; Gloria; Pref. P 64-65, pp. 716-717

4. **Sun. THIRD SUNDAY OF EASTER**
ALL **441**; Gloria, Creed; Pref. P 21-25, pp. **85-87**

5. Mon. Monday of the 3rd Week of Easter
ALL 838; Pref. P 21-25, pp. 704-706

6. Tue. Tuesday of the 3rd Week of Easter
ALL 841; Pref. P 21-25, pp. 704-706

7. Wed. Wednesday of the 3rd Week of Easter
ALL 844; Pref. P 21-25, pp. 704-706

8. Thu. Thursday of the 3rd Week of Easter
ALL 848; Pref. P 21-25, pp. 704-706

9. Fri. Friday of the 3rd Week of Easter
ALL 851; Pref. P 21-25, pp. 704-706

10. Sat. Saturday of the 3rd Week of Easter
ALL 855; Pref. P 21-25, pp. 704-706

OR: St. Damien de Veuster, Pr (1049)
AP 1138-1143; RC 855; Pref. P 21-25, pp. 704-706

11. **Sun. FOURTH SUNDAY OF EASTER**
ALL **448**; Gloria, Creed; Pref. P 21-25, pp. **85-87**

12. Mon. Monday of the 4th Week of Easter
ALL 858; Pref. P 21-25, pp. 704-706

OR: Sts. Nereus & Achilleus, Mm (1050)
AP 1104-1111 or 1115-1118; RC 859; Pref. P 21-25, pp. 704-706

OR: St. Pancras, M (1051)
AP 1112-1115 or 1118-1121; RC 859; Pref. P 21-25, pp. 704-706

13. Tue. Tuesday of the 4th Week of Easter
ALL 863; Pref. P 21-25, pp. 704-706

OR: Our Lady of Fatima (1051)
AP 1090; RC 864; Pref. P 56-57, pp. 715-716

14. Wed. ST. MATTHIAS, APOSTLE (F) (1052)
ALL 1052; Gloria; Pref. P 64-65, pp. 716-717

15. Thu. Thursday of the 4th Week of Easter
ALL 870; Pref. P 21-25, pp. 704-706

OR: St. Isidore (1056)
AP 1158-1160; RC 870; Pref. P 21-25, pp. 704-706

16. Fri. Friday of the 4th Week of Easter
ALL 873; Pref. P 21-25, pp. 704-706

17. Sat. Saturday of the 4th Week of Easter
ALL 876; Pref. P 21-25, pp. 704-706

18. **Sun. FIFTH SUNDAY OF EASTER**
ALL **454**; Gloria, Creed; Pref. P 21-25, pp. **85-87**

19. Mon. Monday of the 5th Week of Easter
ALL 880; Pref. P 21-25, pp. 704-706

20. Tue. Tuesday of the 5th Week of Easter
ALL 883; Pref. P 21-25, pp. 704-706

OR: St. Bernardine of Siena, Pr (1057)
AP 1138-1143 or 1164-1166; RC 884; Pref. P 21-25, pp. 704-706

21. Wed. Wednesday of the 5th Week of Easter
ALL 887; Pref. P 21-25, pp. 704-706

OR: St. Christopher Magallanes, Pr, & Comps, Mm (1058)
AP 1104-1111 or 1115-1118; RC 887; Pref. P 21-25, pp. 704-706

22. Thu. Thursday of the 5th Week of Easter
ALL 890; Pref. P 21-25, pp. 704-706

OR: St. Rita of Cascia, Rel (1059)
AP 1164-1166; RC 891; Pref. P 21-25, pp. 704-706

23. Fri. Friday of the 5th Week of Easter
ALL 893; Pref. P 21-25, pp. 704-706

24. Sat. Saturday of the 5th Week of Easter
ALL 897; Pref. P 21-25, pp. 704-706

25. **Sun. SIXTH SUNDAY OF EASTER**
ALL **460**; Gloria, Creed; Pref. P 21-25, pp. **85-87**

26. Mon. St. Philip Neri, Pr (Mem) (1062)
AP 1062; RC 900; Pref. P 21-25, pp. 704-706

27. Tue. Tuesday of the 6th Week of Easter
ALL 903; Pref. P 21-25, pp. 704-706

OR: St. Augustine of Canterbury (1063)
AP 1138-1143 or 1128-1131; RC 903; Pref. P 21-25, pp. 704-706

28. Wed. Wednesday of the 6th Week of Easter
ALL 906; Pref. P 21-25, pp. 704-706

EVENING: **VIGIL MASS OF THE ASCENSION OF THE LORD (Sol)**
ALL **466**; Gloria; Creed; Pref. P 26-27, pp. **87-88**

29. **Thu. THE ASCENSION OF THE LORD (Sol) (Holyday of Obligation)**
ALL **473**; Gloria, Creed; Pref. P 26-27, pp. **87-88**

30. Fri. Friday of the 6th Week of Easter
ALL 913; Pref. P 26-27, p. 707

31. Sat. THE VISITATION OF THE BVM (F)
ALL 1064; Gloria; Pref. P 57, p. 715

JUNE

1. **Sun. SEVENTH SUNDAY OF EASTER**
ALL **475**; Gloria, Creed; Pref. P 21-25, pp. **85-87** or P 26-27, pp. **87-88**

WHERE THE ASCENSION IS NOT TO BE OBSERVED AS A HOLYDAY OF OBLIGATION, IT IS ASSIGNED TO THE SEVENTH SUNDAY OF EASTER. **The specified rubrics below are to be followed until Monday of the 7th Week of Easter.**

29. Thu. Thursday of the 6th Week of Easter
ALL 909; Pref. P 21-25, pp. 704-706

30. Fri. Friday of the 6th Week of Easter
ALL 913; Collect: *Hear our prayers, O Lord*;
Pref. P 21-25, pp. 704-706

31. Sat. THE VISITATION OF THE BVM (F)
ALL 1064; Gloria; Pref. P 57, p. 715

EVENING: **VIGIL MASS OF THE ASCENSION OF THE LORD (Sol)**
ALL **466**; Gloria, Creed; Pref. P 26-27, pp. **87-88**

JUNE

1. **Sun. ASCENSION OF THE LORD (Sol)**
ALL **473**; Gloria, Creed; Pref. 26-27, pp. **87-88**

2. Mon. Monday of the 7th Week of Easter
ALL 920; Pref. P 21-27, pp. 704-707

OR: Sts. Marcellinus & Peter, Mm (1073)
AP 1104-1112 or 1115-1118; RC 921; Pref. P 21-27, pp. 704-707

3. Tue. Sts. Charles Lwanga & Comps, Mm (Mem) (1074)
AP 1074; RC 924; Pref. P 21-27, pp. 704-707

4. Wed. Wednesday of the 7th Week of Easter
ALL 927; Pref. P 21-27, pp. 704-707

5. Thu. St. Boniface, B & M (Mem) (1075)
AP 1112-1115 or 1118-1119 or 1138-1143; RC 931; Pref. P 21-27, pp. 704-707

OR: Mass of Our Lord Jesus Christ, the Eternal High Priest (1st Thu.)
AP 1348-1349; RC 931; Pref. P 47-48, pp. 711-712

6. Fri. Friday of the 7th Week of Easter
ALL 934; Pref. P 21-27, pp. 704-707

OR: St. Norbert, B (1076)
AP 1128-1131 or 1164-1166; RC 934; Pref. P 21-27, pp. 704-707

OR: Mass of the Most Sacred Heart of Jesus (1st Fri.)
AP 1352-1354; RC 934; Pref. P 45, p. 1353

7. Sat. Saturday of the 7th Week of Easter
ALL 937; Pref. P 21-27, pp. 704-707

OR: Mass of the Immaculate Heart of the BVM (1st Sat.)
AP 1069-1071; RC 938; Pref. P 56-57, pp. 715-716

EVENING: **VIGIL MASS OF PENTECOST (Sol)**
ALL **481**; Gloria, Creed; Pref. P 28, p. **496**

8. **Sun. PENTECOST SUNDAY (Sol)**
ALL **490**; Gloria, Creed

VOLUME II
June 9 to November 29, 2014

---

9. Mon. Monday of the 10th Week in Ordinary Time*
AP 29 (10th Week) or (1st-34th Week) 17-63
RC 788 (II); Pref. P 37-42, pp. 689-692

OR: St. Ephrem, Deacon & D (437)
AP 1104-1106; RC 788 (II); Pref. P 37-42, pp. 689-692

10. Tue. Tuesday of the 10th Week in Ordinary Time*
AP 29 (10th Week) or (1st-34th Week) 17-63
RC 789 (II); Pref. P 37-42, pp. 689-692

11. Wed. St. Barnabas, Apostle (Mem) (438)
ALL 438; Pref. P 64-65, pp. 697-698

12. Thu. Thursday of the 10th Week in Ordinary Time*
AP 29 (10th Week) or (1st-34th Week) 17-63
RC 793 (II); Pref. P 37-42, pp. 689-692

13. Fri. St. Anthony of Padua, Pr & D (Mem) (442)
AP 1093-1095 or 1104-1106 or 1124-1126
RC 794 (II); Pref. P 37-42, pp. 689-692

14. Sat. Saturday of the 10th Week in Ordinary Time*
AP 29 (10th Week) or (1st-34th Week) 17-63
RC 796 (II); Pref. P 37-42, pp. 689-692

OR: Mass of the BVM on Saturday
AP 1050-1059; RC 796 (II); Pref. P 56-57, pp. 695-696

15. **Sun. THE MOST HOLY TRINITY (Sol)**
ALL **499**; Gloria, Creed; Pref. P 43, p. **503**

16. Mon. Monday of the 11th Week in Ordinary Time*
AP 30 (11th Week) or (1st-34th Week) 17-63
RC 797 (II); Pref. P 37-42, pp. 689-692

17. Tue. Tuesday of the 11th Week in Ordinary Time*
AP 30 (11th Week) or (1st-34th Week) 17-63
RC 799 (II); Pref. P 37-42, pp. 689-692

18. Wed. Wednesday of the 11th Week in Ordinary Time*
AP 30 (11th Week) or (1st-34th Week) 17-63
RC 801 (II); Pref. P 37-42, pp. 689-692

19. Thu. Thursday of the 11th Week in Ordinary Time*
AP 30 (11th Week) or (1st-34th Week) 17-63
RC 802 (II); Pref. P 37-42, pp. 689-692

OR: St. Romuald, Ab (442)
AP 1120-1121; RC 802 (II); Pref. P 37-42, pp. 689-692

20. Fri. Friday of the 11th Week in Ordinary Time*
AP 30 (11th Week) or (1st-34th Week) 17-63
RC 804 (II); Pref. P 37-42, pp. 689-692

21. Sat. St. Aloysius Gonzaga, Rel (Mem) (443)
AP 443; RC 807 (II); Pref. P 37-42, pp. 689-692

22. **Sun. THE MOST HOLY BODY AND BLOOD OF CHRIST (Corpus Christi) (Sol)**
ALL **505**; Gloria, Creed; Pref. 47-48, pp. **92-93**

23. Mon. Monday of the 12th Week in Ordinary Time*
AP 31 (12th Week) or (1st-34th Week) 17-63
RC 809 (II); Pref. P 37-42, pp. 689-692

EVENING: VIGIL MASS OF THE NATIVITY OF ST. JOHN THE BAPTIST (Sol)
ALL 447 (**1421**); Gloria, Creed

24. Tue. THE NATIVITY OF ST. JOHN THE BAPTIST (Sol)
ALL 452 (**1426**); Gloria, Creed; Pref. P 61, p. 455 (p. **1430**)

25. Wed. Wednesday of the 12th Week in Ordinary Time*
AP 31 (12th Week) or (1st-34th Week) 17-63
RC 812 (II); Pref. P 37-42, pp. 689-692

26. Thu. Thursday of the 12th Week in Ordinary Time*
AP 31 (12th Week) or (1st-34th Week) 17-63
RC 814 (II); Pref. P 37-42, pp. 689-692

27. Fri. THE MOST SACRED HEART OF JESUS (Sol)
ALL 3; Gloria, Creed; Pref. P 45, p. 7

28. Sat. The Immaculate Heart of the Blessed Virgin Mary (Mem) (430)
ALL 430; Pref. P 56 (on the feast day) or Pref. P 57, pp. 695-696

EVENING: VIGIL MASS OF STS. PETER & PAUL, APOSTLES (Sol)
ALL 459 (**1432**); Gloria, Creed; Pref. P 63, p. 467 (p. **1441**)

29. **STS. PETER & PAUL, APOSTLES (Sol)**
ALL **1437**; Gloria, Creed; Pref. P 63, p. **1441**

30. Mon. Monday of the 13th Week in Ordinary Time*
AP 33 (13th Week) or (1st-34th Week) 17-63
RC 821 (II); Pref. P 37-42, pp. 689-692

OR: The First Martyrs of Holy Roman Church (468)
AP 1064-1071; RC 821 (II); Pref. P 37-42, pp. 689-692

JULY

1. Tue. Tuesday of the 13th Week in Ordinary Time*
AP 33 (13th Week) or (1st-34th Week) 17-63
RC 823 (II); Pref. P 37-42, pp. 689-692

OR: Bl. Junípero Serra, Pr (469)
AP 1098-1103 or 1093-1095; RC 823 (II); Pref. P 37-42, pp. 689-692

2. Wed. Wednesday of the 13th Week in Ordinary Time*
AP 33 (13th Week) or (1st-34th Week) 17-63
RC 824 (II); Pref. P 37-42, pp. 689-692

3. Thu. ST. THOMAS, APOSTLE (F)
ALL 470; Gloria, Creed; Pref. P 64-65, pp. 697-698

OR: Mass of Our Lord Jesus Christ, the Eternal High Priest (1st Thu.)
AP 1308-1309; RC 826 (II); Pref. P 47-48, pp. 692-693

4. Fri. Friday of the 13th Week in Ordinary Time*
AP 33 (13th Week) or (1st-34th Week) 17-63
RC 828 (II); Pref. P 37-42, pp. 689-692

OR: Independence Day
ALL 473; Gloria, Pref. P 82-83, pp. 476-478

OR: Mass of the Most Sacred Heart of Jesus (1st Fri.)
AP 1312-1314; RC 828 (II); Pref. P 45, p. 1313

5. Sat. Saturday of the 13th Week in Ordinary Time*
AP 33 (13th Week) or (1st-34th Week) 17-63
RC 829 (II); Pref. P 37-42, pp. 689-692

OR: St. Anthony Zaccaria, Pr (479)
AP 1093-1095 or 1128-1129 or 1124-1126
RC 829 (II); Pref. P 37-42, pp. 689-692

OR: St. Elizabeth of Portugal (479)
AP 1127-1128; RC 829 (II); Pref. P 37-42, pp. 689-692

OR: Mass of the Immaculate Heart of the BVM (1st Sat.)
AP 430-432; RC 829 (II); Pref. P 56-57, pp. 695-696

OR: Mass of the BVM of Saturday (1st Sat.)
AP 1050-1059; RC 829 (II); Pref. P 56-57, pp. 695-696

6. **Sun. FOURTEENTH SUNDAY IN ORDINARY TIME**
ALL **535**; Gloria, Creed; Pref. P 29-36, pp. **88-92**
7. Mon. Monday of the 14th Week in Ordinary Time*
AP 34 (14th Week) or (1st-34th Week) 17-63
RC 831 (II); Pref. P 37-42, pp. 689-692
8. Tue. Tuesday of the 14th Week in Ordinary Time*
AP 34 (14th Week) or (1st-34th Week) 17-63
RC 832 (II); Pref. P 37-42, pp. 689-692
9. Wed. Wednesday of the 14th Week in Ordinary Time*
AP 34 (14th Week) or (1st-34th Week) 17-63
RC 834 (II); Pref. P 37-42, pp. 689-692

OR: St. Augustine Zhao Rong, Pr, & Comps, Mm (481)
AP 1064-1071; RC 834 (II); Pref. P 37-42, pp. 689-692

10. Thu. Thursday of the 14th Week in Ordinary*
AP 34 (14th Week) or (1st-34th Week) 17-63
RC 836 (II); Pref. P 37-42, pp. 689-692
11. Fri. St. Benedict, Ab (Mem) (482)
AP 482; RC 837 (II) (RI 483); Pref. P 37-42, pp. 689-692
12. Sat. Saturday of the 14th Week in Ordinary Time*
AP 34 (14th Week) or (1st-34th Week) 17-63
RC 839 (II); Pref. P 37-42, pp. 689-692

OR: Mass of the BVM on Saturday
AP 1050-1059; RC 839 (II); Pref. P 56-57, pp. 695-696

13. **Sun. FIFTEENTH SUNDAY IN ORDINARY TIME**
ALL **540**; Gloria, Creed; Pref. P 29-36, pp. **88-92**
14. Mon. St. Kateri Tekakwitha, V (Mem) (485)
AP 1108-1112; RC 843 (II); Pref. P 37-42, pp. 689-692
15. Tue. St. Bonaventure, B & D (Mem) (485)
AP 1088-1091 or 1104-1106; RC 844 (II); Pref. P 37-42, pp. 689-692
16. Wed. Wednesday of the 15th Week in Ordinary Time*
AP 36 (15th Week) or (1st-34th Week) 17-63
RC 846 (II); Pref. P 37-42, pp. 689-692

OR: Our Lady of Mount Carmel (486)
AP 1050-1059; RC 846 (II); Pref. P 56-57, pp. 695-696

17. Thu. Thursday of the 15th Week in Ordinary Time*
AP 36 (15th Week) or (1st-34th Week) 17-63
RC 848 (II); Pref. P 37-42, pp. 689-692

18. Fri. Friday of the 15th Week in Ordinary Time*
AP 36 (15th Week) or (1st-34th Week) 17-63
RC 850 (II); Pref. P 37-42, pp. 689-692

OR: St. Camillus de Lellis, Pr (487) **(transferred from 7/14)**
AP 1127-1128; RC 850 (II); Pref. P 37-42, pp. 689-692

19. Sat. Saturday of the 15th Week in Ordinary Time*
AP 36 (15th Week) or (1st-34th Week) 17-63
RC 851 (II); Pref. P 37-42, pp. 689-692

OR: Mass of the BVM on Saturday
AP 1050-1059; RC 851 (II), Pref. P 56-57, pp. 695-696

20. **Sun. SIXTEENTH SUNDAY IN ORDINARY TIME**
ALL **547**; Gloria, Creed; Pref. P 29-36, pp. **88-92**

21. Mon. Monday of the 16th Week in Ordinary Time*
AP 37 (16th Week) or (1st-34th Week) 17-63
RC 853 (II); Pref. P 37-42, pp. 689-692

OR: St. Lawrence of Brindisi, Pr & D (488)
AP 1093-1095 or 1104-1106 or 1124-1126
RC 853 (II); Pref. P 37-42, pp. 689-692

22. Tue. St. Mary Magdalene (Mem) (489)
ALL 489; Pref. P 37-42, pp. 689-692

23. Wed. Wednesday of the 16th Week in Ordinary Time*
AP 37 (16th Week) or (1st-34th Week) 17-63
RC 856 (II); Pref. P 37-42, pp. 689-692

OR: St. Bridget, Rel (493)
AP 1130-1132; RC 856 (II); Pref. P 37-42, pp. 689-692

24. Thu. Thursday of the 16th Week in Ordinary Time
AP 37 (16th Week) or (1st-34th Week) 17-63
RC 858 (II); Pref. P 37-42, pp. 689-692

OR: St. Sharbel Makhlūf, Pr (493)
AP 1093-1095 or 1121-1122
RC 858 (II); Pref. P 37-42, pp. 689-692

25. Fri. ST. JAMES, APOSTLE (F)
ALL 494; Gloria; Pref. P 64-65, pp. 697-698

26. Sat. Sts. Joachim & Anne, Parents of the BVM (Mem) (498)
ALL 498; Pref. P 37-42, pp. 689-692

27. **Sun. SEVENTEENTH SUNDAY IN ORDINARY TIME**
ALL **553**; Gloria, Creed; Pref. P 29-36, pp. **88-92**

28. Mon. Monday of the 17th Week in Ordinary Time*
AP 38 (17th Week) or (1st-34th Week) 17-63
RC 863 (II); Pref. P 37-42, pp. 689-692

29. Tue. St. Martha (Mem) (501)
AP 501; RC 864 (II); Pref. P 37-42, pp. 689-692

30. Wed. Wednesday of the 17th Week in Ordinary Time*
AP 38 (17th Week) or (1st-34th Week) 17-63
RC 866 (II); Pref. P 37-42, pp. 689-692

OR: St. Peter Chrysologus, B & D (503)
AP 1088-1091 or 1104-1106
RC 866 (II); Pref. P 37-42, pp. 689-692

31. Thu. St. Ignatius of Loyola, Pr (Mem) (504)
AP 504; RC 868 (RI 504); Pref. P 37-42, pp. 689-692

AUGUST

1. Fri. St. Alphonsus Liguori, B & D (Mem) (505)
AP 1088-1091 or 1104-1106; Prayers 506-507
RC 869 (II); Pref. P 37-42, pp. 689-692

OR: Mass of the Most Sacred Heart of Jesus (1st Fri.)
AP 1312-1314; RC 869 (II); Pref. P 45, p. 1313

2. Sat. Saturday of the 17th Week in Ordinary Time*
AP 38 (17th Week) or (1st-34th Week) 17-63
RC 871 (II); Pref. P 37-42, pp. 689-692

OR: St. Eusebius of Vercelli, B (507)
AP 1088-1091; RC 871 (II); Pref. P 37-42, pp. 689-692

OR: St. Peter Julian Eymard, Pr (508)
AP 1124-1126 or 1093-1095
RC 871 (II); Pref. P 37-42, pp. 689-692

OR: Mass of the Immaculate Heart of the BVM (1st Sat.)
AP 430-432; RC 871 (II); Pref. P 56-57, pp. 695-696

OR: Mass of the BVM on Saturday
AP 1050-1059; RC 871 (II); Pref. P 56-57, pp. 695-696

3. **Sun. EIGHTEENTH SUNDAY IN ORDINARY TIME**
ALL **558**; Gloria, Creed; Pref. P 29-36, pp. **88-92**

4. Mon. St. John Vianney, Pr (Mem) (508)
AP 1093-1095; RC 872 (II); Pref. P 37-42, pp. 689-692

5. Tue. Tuesday of the 18th Week in Ordinary Time*
AP 40 (18th Week) or (1st-34th Week) 17-63
RC 874 (II); Pref. P 37-42, pp. 689-692

OR: The Dedication of the Basilica of St. Mary Major (510)
AP 1050-1059; RC 874 (II); Pref. P 56-57, pp. 695-696

6. Wed. THE TRANSFIGURATION OF THE LORD (F)
ALL 510 (**1443**); Gloria; G 513 (Year A) (**1446**)

7. Thu. Thursday of the 18th Week in Ordinary Time*
AP 40 (18th Week) or (1st-34th Week) 17-63
RC 878 (II); Pref. P 37-42, pp. 689-692

OR: St. Sixtus II, Po, & Comps, Mm (517)
AP 1064-1071; RC 878 (II); Pref. P 37-42, pp. 689-692

OR: St. Cajetan, Pr (517)
AP 1093-1095 or 1124-1126
RC 878 (II); Pref. P 37-42, pp. 689-692

OR: Mass of Our Lord Jesus Christ, the Eternal High Priest (1st Thu.)
AP 1308-1309; RC 878 (II); Pref. P 47-48, pp. 692-693

8. Fri. St. Dominic, Pr (Mem) (519)
AP 519; RC 880 (II); Pref. P 37-42, pp. 689-692

9. Sat. Saturday of the 18th Week in Ordinary Time*
AP 40 (18th Week) or (1st-34th Week) 17-63
RC 881 (II); Pref. P 37-42, pp. 689-692

OR: St. Teresa Benedicta of the Cross, V & M (520)
AP 1082-1083 or 1108-1112
RC 881 (II); Pref. P 37-42, pp. 689-692

OR: Mass of the BVM on Saturday
AP 1050-1059; RC 881 (II); Pref. P 56-57, pp. 695-696

10. **Sun. NINETEENTH SUNDAY IN ORDINARY TIME**
ALL **564**; Gloria, Creed; Pref. P 29-36, pp. **88-92**

11. Mon. St. Clare, V (Mem) (524)
AP 1108-1112 or 1123-1124
RC 883 (II); Pref. P 37-42, pp. 689-692

12. Tue. Tuesday of the 19th Week in Ordinary Time*
AP 41 (19th Week) or (1st-34th Week) 17-63
RC 885 (II); Pref. P 37-42, pp. 689-692

OR: St. Jane Frances de Chantal, Rel (524)
AP 1124-1126; RC 885 (II); Pref. P 37-42, pp. 689-692

13. Wed. Wednesday of the 19th Week in Ordinary Time*
AP 41 (19th Week) or (1st-34th Week) 17-63
RC 886 (II); Pref. P 37-42, pp. 689-692

OR: Sts. Pontian, Po, & Hippolytus, Pr, Mm (525)
AP 1064-1071 or 1091-1092
RC 886 (II); Pref. P 37-42, pp. 689-692

14. Thu. St. Maximilian Kolbe, Pr & M (Mem) (526)
AP 526; RC 888 (G 527); Pref. P 37-42, pp. 689-692

EVENING: **VIGIL MASS OF THE ASSUMPTION OF THE BVM (Sol)**
ALL **1451**; Gloria, Creed; Pref. P 59, p. **1460**

15. **Fri. ASSUMPTION OF THE BVM (Sol) (Holyday of Obligation)**
ALL **1456**; Gloria, Creed; Pref. P 59, p. **1460**

16. Sat. Saturday of the 19th Week in Ordinary Time*
AP 41 (19th Week) or (1st-34th Week) 17-63
RC 892 (II); Pref. P 37-42, pp. 689-692

OR: St. Stephen of Hungary (528)
AP 1118-1120; RC 892 (II); Pref. P 37-42, pp. 689-692

OR: Mass of the BVM on Saturday
AP 1050-1059; RC 892 (II); Pref. P 56-57, pp. 695-696

17. **Sun. TWENTIETH SUNDAY IN ORDINARY TIME**
ALL **570**; Gloria, Creed; Pref. P 29-36, pp. **88-92**

18. Mon. Monday of the 20th Week in Ordinary Time*
AP 43 (20th Week) or (1st-34th Week) 17-63
RC 899 (II); Pref. P 37-42, pp. 689-692

19. Tue. Tuesday of the 20th Week in Ordinary Time*
AP 43 (20th Week) or (1st-34th Week) 17-63
RC 900 (II); Pref. P 37-42, pp. 689-692

OR: St. John Eudes, Pr (529)
AP 1093-1095 or 1124-1126
RC 900 (II); Pref. P 37-42, pp. 689-692

20. Wed. St. Bernard, Ab & D (Mem) (529)
AP 530; RC 902 (II); Pref. P 37-42, pp. 689-692

21. Thu. St. Pius X, Po (Mem) (531)
AP 1085-1088; RC 904 (II); Pref. P 37-42, pp. 689-692

22. Fri. The Queenship of the BVM (Mem) (532)
AP 532; RC 1147-1168 or 905 (II); Pref. P 56-57, pp. 695-696

23. Sat. Saturday of the 20th Week in Ordinary Time*
AP 43 (20th Week) or (1st-34th Week) 17-63
RC 907 (II); Pref. P 37-42, pp. 689-692

OR: St. Rose of Lima, V (533)
AP 1108-1112; RC 907 (II); Pref. P 37-42, pp. 689-692

OR: Mass of the BVM on Saturday
AP 1050-1059; RC 907 (II); Pref. P 56-57, pp. 695-696

24. **Sun. TWENTY-FIRST SUNDAY IN ORDINARY TIME**
ALL **576**; Gloria, Creed; Pref. P 29-36, pp. **88-92**

25. Mon. Monday of the 21st Week in Ordinary Time*
AP 44 (21st Week) or (1st-34th Week) 17-63
RC 909 (II); Pref. P 37-42, pp. 689-692

OR: St. Louis (538)
AP 1118-1120; RC 909 (II); Pref. P 37-42, pp. 689-692

OR: St. Joseph Calasanz, Pr (538)
AP 1128-1129 or 1093-1095
RC 909 (II); Pref. P 37-42, pp. 689-692

26. Tue. Tuesday of the 21st Week in Ordinary Time*
AP 44 (21st Week) or (1st-34th Week) 17-63
RC 910 (II); Pref. P 37-42, pp. 689-692

27. Wed. St. Monica (Mem) (539)
AP 1130-1132; RC 912 (II) (G 540); Pref. P 37-42, pp. 689-692

28. Thu. St. Augustine, B & D (Mem) (540)
AP 541; RC 913 (II); Pref. P 37-42, pp. 689-692

29. Fri. The Passion of St. John the Baptist (Mem) (542)
ALL 542; Pref. P 61, p. 545

30. Sat. Saturday of the 21st Week in Ordinary Time*
AP 44 (21st Week) or (1st-34th Week) 17-63
RC 916 (II); Pref. P 37-42, pp. 689-692

OR: Mass of the BVM on Saturday
AP 1050-1059; RC 916 (II); Pref. P 56-57, pp. 695-696

31. **Sun. TWENTY-SECOND SUNDAY IN ORDINARY TIME**
ALL **582**; Gloria, Creed; Pref. P 29-36, pp. **88-92**

SEPTEMBER

1. Mon. Monday of the 22nd Week in Ordinary Time*
AP 45 (22nd Week) or (1st-34th Week) 17-63
RC 917 (II); Pref. P 37-42, pp. 689-692

OR: Labor Day
AP 1293-1295; RC 917 (II); Pref. P 37-42, pp. 689-612

2. Tue. Tuesday of the 22nd Week in Ordinary Time*
AP 45 (22nd Week) or (1st-34th Week) 17-63
RC 918 (II); Pref. P 37-42, pp. 689-692

3. Wed. St. Gregory the Great, Po & D (Mem) (546)
AP 546; RC 920 (II); Pref. P 37-42, pp. 689-692

4. Thu. Thursday of the 22nd Week in Ordinary Time*
AP 45 (22nd Week) or (1st-34th Week) 17-63
RC 921 (II); Pref. P 37-42, pp. 689-692

OR: Mass of Our Lord Jesus Christ, the Eternal High Priest (1st Thu.)
AP 1308-1309; RC 921 (II); Pref. P 47-48, pp. 692-693

5. Fri. Friday of the 22nd Week in Ordinary Time*
AP 45 (22nd Week) or (1st-34th Week) 17-63
RC 923 (II); Pref. P 37-42, pp. 689-692

OR: Mass of the Most Sacred Heart of Jesus (1st Fri.)
AP 1312-1314; RC 923 (II); Pref. P 45, p. 1313

6. Sat. Saturday of the 22nd Week in Ordinary Time*
AP 45 (22nd Week) or (1st-34th Week) 17-63
RC 924 (II); Pref. P 37-42, pp. 689-692

OR: Mass of the Immaculate Heart of the BVM (1st Sat.)
AP 430-432; RC 924 (II); Pref. P 56-57, pp. 695-696

OR: Mass of the BVM on Saturday
AP 1050-1059; RC 924 (II); Pref. P 56-57, pp. 695-696

7. **Sun. TWENTY-THIRD SUNDAY IN ORDINARY TIME**
ALL **587**; Gloria, Creed; Pref. P 29-36, pp. **88-92**

8. Mon. The Nativity of the Blessed Virgin Mary (F) (548)
ALL 548; Gloria; Pref. P 56-57, pp. 695-696

9. Tue. St. Peter Claver, Pr (Mem) (553)
AP 1093-1095 or 1127-1128
RC 927 (II); Pref. P 37-42, pp. 689-692

10. Wed. Wednesday of the 23rd Week in Ordinary Time*
AP 47 (23rd Week) or (1st-34th Week) 17-63
RC 929 (II); Pref. P 37-42, pp. 689-692

11. Thu. Thursday of the 23rd Week in Ordinary Time*
AP 47 (23rd Week) or (1st-34th Week) 17-63
RC 930 (II); Pref. P 37-42, pp. 689-692

12. Fri. Friday of the 23rd Week in Ordinary Time*
AP 47 (23rd Week) or (1st-34th Week) 17-63
RC 932 (II); Pref. P 37-42, pp. 689-692

OR: The Most Holy Name of Mary (554)
AP 554; RC 932 (II); Pref. P 37-42, pp. 689-692

13. Sat. St. John Chrysostom, B & D (Mem) (555)
AP 555; RC 934 (II); Pref. P 37-42, pp. 689-692

14. **Sun. THE EXALTATION OF THE HOLY CROSS (F)**
ALL **1462**; Gloria, Creed; Pref. P 46, p. **1466**

15. Mon. Our Lady of Sorrows (Mem) (562)
ALL 562; Pref. P 56-57, pp. 695-696

16. Tue. Sts. Cornelius, Po, & Cyprian, B, Mm (Mem) (568)
AP 1064-1071 or 1088-1091; Prayers 568
RC 937 (II); Pref. P 37-42, pp. 689-692

17. Wed. Wednesday of the 24th Week in Ordinary Time*
AP 48 (24th Week) or (1st-34th Week) 17-63
RC 938 (II); Pref. P 37-42, pp. 689-692

OR: St. Robert Bellarmine, B & D (569)
AP 1088-1091 or 1104-1106; RC 938 (II); Pref. P 37-42, pp. 689-692

18. Thu. Thursday of the 24th Week in Ordinary Time*
AP 48 (24th Week) or (1st-34th Week) 17-63
RC 940 (II); Pref. P 37-42, pp. 689-692

19. Fri. Friday of the 24th Week in Ordinary Time*
AP 48 (24th Week) or (1st-34th Week) 17-63
RC 941 (II); Pref. P 37-42, pp. 689-692

OR: St. Januarius, B & M (570)
AP 1072-1075 or 1088-1091
RC 941 (II); Pref. P 37-42, pp. 689-692

20. Sat. Sts. Andrew Kim Tae-gŏn, Pr, & Paul Chŏng Ha-sang, & Comps, Mm (Mem) (570)
AP 571; RC 942 (II); Pref. P 37-42, pp. 689-692

21. **Sun. TWENTY-FIFTH SUNDAY IN ORDINARY TIME**
ALL **599**; Gloria, Creed; Pref. P 29-36, pp. **88-92**

22. Mon. Monday of the 25th Week in Ordinary Time*
AP 50 (25th Week) or (1st-34th Week) 17-63
RC 947 (II); Pref. P 37-42, pp. 689-692

23. Tue. St. Pius of Pietrelcina, Pr (Mem) (575)
AP 1093-1095 or 1124-1126; RC 948 (II);
Pref. P 37-42, pp. 689-692

24. Wed. Wednesday of the 25th Week in Ordinary Time*
AP 50 (25th Week) or (1st-34th Week) 17-63
RC 950 (II); Pref. P 37-42, pp. 689-692

25. Thu. Thursday of the 25th Week in Ordinary Time*
AP 50 (25th Week) or (1st-34th Week) 17-63
RC 951 (II); Pref. P 37-42, pp. 689-692

26. Fri. Friday of the 25th Week in Ordinary Time*
AP 50 (25th Week) or (1st-34th Week) 17-63
RC 953 (II); Pref. P 37-42, pp. 689-692

OR: Sts. Cosmas & Damian, Mm (576)
AP 1064-1071; RC 953 (II); Pref. P 37-42, pp. 689-692

27. Sat. St. Vincent de Paul, Pr (Mem) (577)
AP 577; RC 954 (II); Pref. P 37-42, pp. 689-692

28. **Sun. TWENTY-SIXTH SUNDAY IN ORDINARY TIME**
ALL **605**; Gloria, Creed; Pref. P 29-36, pp. **88-92**

29. Mon. STS. MICHAEL, GABRIEL, & RAPHAEL, ARCHANGELS (F)
ALL 580; Gloria; Pref. P 60, p. 697

30. Tue. St. Jerome, Pr & D (Mem) (584)
AP 584; RC 958 (II) (RI 585); Pref. P 37-42, pp. 689-692

OCTOBER

1. Wed. St. Thérèse of the Child Jesus, V & D (Mem) (586)
ALL 586; Pref. P 37-42, pp. 689-692

2. Thu. The Holy Guardian Angels (Mem) (588)
ALL 588; Pref. P 60, p. 697

OR: Mass of Our Lord Jesus Christ, the Eternal High Priest (1st Thu.)
AP 1308-1309; RC 589; Pref. P 47-48, pp. 692-693

3. Fri. Friday of the 26th Week in Ordinary Time*
AP 51 (26th Week) or (1st-34th Week) 17-63
RC 963 (II); Pref. P 37-42, pp. 689-692

OR: Mass of the Most Sacred Heart of Jesus (1st Fri.)
AP 1312-1314; RC 963 (II); Pref. P 45, p. 1313

4. Sat. St. Francis of Assisi (Mem) (591)
AP 592; RC 965 (II) (RI 592); Pref. P 37-42, pp. 689-692

5. **Sun. TWENTY-SEVENTH SUNDAY IN ORDINARY TIME**
ALL **611**; Gloria, Creed; Pref. P 29-36, pp. **88-92**

6. Mon. Monday of the 27th Week in Ordinary Time*
AP 52 (27th Week) or (1st-34th Week) 17-63
RC 966 (II); Pref. P 37-42, pp. 689-692

OR: St. Bruno, Pr (593)
AP 1121-1124 or 1093-1095
RC 966 (II); Pref. P 37-42, pp. 689-692

OR: Bl. Marie Rose Durocher, V (594)
AP 1108-1112; RC 966 (II); Pref. P 37-42, pp. 689-692

7. Tue. Our Lady of the Rosary (Mem) (595)
AP 595; RC 1147-1168 or 968 (II); Pref. P 56-57, pp. 695-696

8. Wed. Wednesday of the 27th Week in Ordinary Time*
AP 52 (27th Week) or (1st-34th Week) 17-63
RC 969 (II); Pref. P 37-42, pp. 689-692

9. Thu. Thursday of the 27th Week in Ordinary Time*
AP 52 (27th Week) or (1st-34th Week) 17-63
RC 971 (II); Pref. P 37-42, pp. 689-692

OR: St. Denis, B & Comps, Mm (596)
AP 1064-1071; RC 971 (II); Pref. P 37-42, pp. 689-692

OR: St. John Leonardi, Pr (597)
AP 1098-1103 or 1127-1128
RC 971 (II); Pref. P 37-42, pp. 689-692

10. Fri. Friday of the 27th Week in Ordinary Time*
AP 52 (27th Week) or (1st-34th Week) 17-63
RC 972 (II); Pref. P 37-42, pp. 689-692

11. Sat. Saturday of the 27th Week in Ordinary Time*
AP 52 (27th Week) or (1st-34th Week) 17-63
RC 973 (II); Pref. P 37-42, pp. 689-692

OR: Mass of the BVM on Saturday
AP 1050-1059; RC 973 (II); Pref. P 56-57, pp. 695-696

12. **Sun. TWENTY-EIGHTH SUNDAY IN ORDINARY TIME**
ALL **617**; Gloria, Creed; Pref. P 29-36, pp. **88-92**

13. Mon. Monday of the 28th Week in Ordinary Time*
AP 54 (28th Week) or (1st-34th Week) 17-63
RC 975 (II); Pref. P 37-42, pp. 689-692

14. Tue. Tuesday of the 28th Week in Ordinary Time*
AP 54 (28th Week) or (1st-34th Week) 17-63
RC 976 (II); Pref. P 37-42, pp. 689-692

OR: St. Callistus I, Po & M (598)
AP 1072-1075 or 1085-1088
RC 976 (II); Pref. P 37-42, pp. 689-692

15. Wed. St. Teresa of Jesus, V & D (Mem) (598)
AP 599; RC 977 (II) (RI 599); Pref. P 37-42, pp. 689-692

16. Thu. Thursday of the 28th Week in Ordinary Time*
AP 54 (28th Week) or (1st-34th Week) 17-63
RC 979 (II); Pref. P 37-42, pp. 689-692

OR: St. Hedwig, Rel (600)
AP 1124-1126 or 1130-1132
RC 979 (II); Pref. P 37-42, pp. 689-692

OR: St. Margaret Mary Alacoque, V (601)
AP 1108-1112; RC 979 (II); Pref. P 37-42, pp. 689-692

17. Fri. St. Ignatius of Antioch, B & M (Mem) (602)
AP 602; RC 980 (II); Pref. P 37-42, pp. 689-692

18. Sat. ST. LUKE, EVANGELIST (F)
ALL 603; Gloria; Pref. P 65, p. 698

19. **Sun. TWENTY-NINTH SUNDAY IN ORDINARY TIME**
ALL **624**; Gloria, Creed; Pref. P 29-36, pp. **88-92**

20. Mon. Monday of the 29th Week in Ordinary Time*
AP 55 (29th Week) or (1st-34th Week) 17-63
RC 983 (II); Pref. P 37-42, pp. 689-692

OR: St. Paul of the Cross, Pr (607)
AP 607; RC 983 (II); Pref. P 37-42, pp. 689-692

21. Tue. Tuesday of the 29th Week in Ordinary Time*
AP 55 (29th Week) or (1st-34th Week) 17-63
RC 984 (II); Pref. P 37-42, pp. 689-692

22. Wed. Wednesday of the 29th Week in Ordinary Time*
AP 55 (29th Week) or (1st-34th Week) 17-63
RC 986 (II); Pref. P 37-42, pp. 689-692

23. Thu. Thursday of the 29th Week in Ordinary Time*
AP 55 (29th Week) or (1st-34th Week) 17-63
RC 987 (II); Pref. P 37-42, pp. 689-692

OR: St. John Capistrano, Pr (609)
AP 1098-1103 or 1124-1126
RC 987 (II); Pref. P 37-42, pp. 689-692

24. Fri. Friday of the 29th Week in Ordinary Time*
AP 55 (29th Week) or (1st-34th Week) 17-63
RC 989 (II); Pref. P 37-42, pp. 689-692

OR: St. Anthony Mary Claret, B (609)
AP 1098-1103 or 1088-1091
RC 989 (II); Pref. P 37-42, pp. 689-692

25. Sat. Saturday of the 29th Week in Ordinary Time*
AP 55 (29th Week) or (1st-34th Week) 17-63
RC 990 (II); Pref. P 37-42, pp. 689-692

OR: Mass of the BVM on Saturday
AP 1050-1059, RC 990 (II); Pref. P 56-57, pp. 695-696

26. **Sun. THIRTIETH SUNDAY IN ORDINARY TIME**
ALL **629**; Gloria, Creed; Pref. P 29-36, pp. **88-92**

27. Mon. Monday of the 30th Week in Ordinary Time*
AP 57 (30th Week) or (1st-34th Week) 17-63
RC 995 (II); Pref. P 37-42, pp. 689-692

28. Tue. STS. SIMON & JUDE, APOSTLES (F)
ALL 610; Gloria; Pref. P 64-65, pp. 697-698

29. Wed. Wednesday of the 30th Week in Ordinary Time*
AP 57 (30th Week) or (1st-34th Week) 17-63
RC 998 (II); Pref. P 37-42, pp. 689-692

30. Thu. Thursday of the 30th Week in Ordinary Time*
AP 57 (30th Week) or (1st-34th Week) 17-63
RC 999 (II); Pref. P 37-42, pp. 689-692

31. Fri. Friday of the 30th Week in Ordinary Time*
AP 57 (30th Week) or (1st-34th Week) 17-63
RC 1000 (II); Pref. P 37-42, pp. 689-692

NOVEMBER

1. **Sat. ALL SAINTS (Sol) (Holyday of Obligation)**
ALL **1468**; Gloria, Creed; Pref. P 72, p. **1473**

2. **Sun. THE COMMEMORATION OF ALL THE FAITHFUL DEPARTED (All Souls' Day)**

1st Mass: ALL **1476**; Pref. P 77-81, pp. **93-95**
2nd Mass: ALL **1481**; Pref. P 77-81, pp. **93-95**
3rd Mass: ALL **1485**; Pref. P 77-81, pp. **93-95**

3. Mon. Monday of the 31st Week in Ordinary Time*
AP 58 (31st Week) or (1st-34th Week) 17-63
RC 1003 (II); Pref. P 37-42, pp. 689-692

OR: St. Martin de Porres, Rel (743)
AP 1124-1126; RC 1003 (II); Pref. P 37-42, pp. 689-692

4. Tue. St. Charles Borromeo, B (Mem) (743)
AP 1088-1091; Prayers 743; RC 1004 (II)
Pref. P 37-42, pp. 689-692

5. Wed. Wednesday of the 31st Week in Ordinary Time*
AP 58 (31st Week) or (1st-34th Week) 17-63
RC 1006 (II); Pref. P 37-42, pp. 689-692

6. Thu. Thursday of the 31st Week in Ordinary Time*
AP 58 (31st Week) or (1st-34th Week) 17-63
RC 1007 (II); Pref. P 37-42, pp. 689-692

OR: Mass of Our Lord Jesus Christ, the Eternal High Priest (1st Thu.)
AP 1308-1309; RC 1007 (II); Pref. P 47-48, pp. 692-693

7. Fri. Friday of the 31st Week in Ordinary Time*
AP 58 (31st Week) or (1st-34th Week) 17-63
RC 1009 (II); Pref. P 37-42, pp. 689-692

OR: Mass of the Most Sacred Heart of Jesus (1st Fri.)
AP 1312-1314; RC 1009 (II); Pref. P 45, p. 1313

8. Sat. Saturday of the 31st Week in Ordinary Time*
AP 58 (31st Week) or (1st-34th Week) 17-63
RC 1010 (II); Pref. P 37-42, pp. 689-692

OR: Mass of the BVM on Saturday
AP 1050-1059; RC 1010 (II); Pref. P 56-57, pp. 695-696

9. **Sun. THE DEDICATION OF THE LATERAN BASILICA (F)**
ALL **1491**; Gloria, Creed; Pref. P 53, p. **1496**

10. Mon. St. Leo the Great, Po & D (749)
AP 749; RC 1012 (II); Pref. P 37-42, pp. 689-692

11. Tue. St. Martin of Tours, B (Mem) (750)
AP 750; RC 1013 (II); Pref. P 37-42, pp. 689-692

12. Wed. St. Josaphat, B & M (Mem) (752)
AP 752; RC 1015 (II); Pref. P 37-42, pp. 689-692

13. Thu. St. Frances Xavier Cabrini, V (Mem) (753)
AP 1108-1112 or 1127-1128
RC 1016 (II); Pref. P 37-42, pp. 689-692

14. Fri. Friday of the 32nd Week in Ordinary Time*
AP 59 (32nd Week) or (1st-34th Week) 17-63
RC 1018 (II); Pref. P 37-42, pp. 689-692

15. Sat. Saturday of the 32nd Week in Ordinary Time*
AP 59 (32nd Week) or (1st-34th Week) 17-63
RC 1019 (II); Pref. P 37-42, pp. 689-692

OR: St. Albert the Great, B & D (754)
AP 1088-1091 or 1104-1106;
RC 1019 (II); Pref. P 37-42, pp. 689-692

OR: Mass of the BVM on Saturday
AP 1050-1059; RC 1019 (II); Pref. P 56-57, pp. 695-696

16. **Sun. THIRTY-THIRD SUNDAY IN ORDINARY TIME**
ALL **647**; Gloria, Creed; Pref. P 29-36, pp. **88-92**

17. Mon. St. Elizabeth of Hungary, Rel (Mem) (756)
AP 1127-1128; RC 1020 (II); Pref. P 37-42, pp. 689-692

18. Tue. Tuesday of the 33rd Week in Ordinary Time*
AP 61 (33rd Week) or (1st-34th Week) 17-63
RC 1022 (II); Pref. P 37-42, pp. 689-692

OR: The Dedication of the Basilicas of Sts. Peter & Paul, Apostles
ALL 756; Pref. P 64-65, pp. 697-698

OR: St. Rose Philippine Duchesne, V (760)
AP 1108-1112; RC 1022 (II); Pref. P 37-42, pp. 689-692

19. Wed. Wednesday of the 33rd Week in Ordinary Time*
AP 61 (33rd Week) or (1st-34th Week) 17-63
RC 1024 (II); Pref. P 37-42, pp. 689-692

20. Thu. Thursday of the 33rd Week in Ordinary Time*
AP 61 (33rd Week) or (1st-34th Week) 17-63
RC 1026 (II); Pref. P 37-42, pp. 689-692

21. Fri. The Presentation of the Blessed Virgin Mary (Mem) (761)
AP 1050-1059; RC 1027 (II); Pref. P 56-57, pp. 695-696

22. Sat. St. Cecilia, V & M (Mem) (762)
AP 1082-1083 or 1108-1112
RC 1029 (II); Pref. P 37-42, pp. 689-692

23. **Sun. OUR LORD JESUS CHRIST, KING OF THE UNIVERSE (Sol)**
ALL **653**; Gloria, Creed; Pref. P 51, p. **658**

24. Mon. St. Andrew Dũng-Lạc, Pr, & Comps, Mm (Mem) (765)
AP 765; RC 1030 (II); Pref. P 37-42, pp. 689-692

25. Tue. Tuesday of the 34th Week in Ordinary Time*
AP 62 (34th Week) or (1st-34th Week) 17-63
RC 1032 (II); Pref. P 37-42, pp. 689-692

OR: St. Catherine of Alexandria, V & M (766)
AP 1082-1083 or 1108-1112; RC 1032 (II)
Pref. P 37-42, pp. 689-692

26. Wed. Wednesday of the 34th Week in Ordinary Time*
AP 62 (34th Week) or (1st-34th Week) 17-63
RC 1033 (II); Pref. P 37-42, pp. 689-692

27. Thu. Thursday of the 34th Week in Ordinary Time*
AP 62 (34th Week) or (1st-34th Week) 17-63
RC 1034 (II); Pref. P 37-42, pp. 689-692

OR: Thanksgiving Day
ALL 770; RC 1034 (II); Pref. P 84, p. 706

28. Fri. Friday of the 34th Week in Ordinary Time*
AP 62 (34th Week) or (1st-34th Week) 17-63
RC 1036 (II); Pref. P 37-42, pp. 689-692

29. Sat. Saturday of the 34th Week in Ordinary Time*
AP 62 (34th Week) or (1st-34th Week) 17-63
RC 1038 (II); Pref. P 37-42, pp. 689-692

OR: Mass of the BVM on Saturday
AP 1050-1059; RC 1038 (II); Pref. P 56-57, pp. 695-696

VOLUME I
November 30 to December 31, 2014

---

30. **Sun. FIRST SUNDAY OF ADVENT**
ALL **666**; Creed; Pref. P 1, p. **82**

DECEMBER

1. Mon. Monday of the 1st Week of Advent
ALL 3; Pref. P 1, p. 699

2. Tue. Tuesday of the 1st Week of Advent
ALL 7; Pref. P 1, p. 699

3. Wed. St. Francis Xavier, Pr (Mem) (948)
AP 948-949; RC 11; Pref. P 1, p. 699

4. Thu. Thursday of the 1st Week of Advent
ALL 14; Pref. P 1, p. 699

OR: St. John Damascene, Pr & D (949)
AP 1133-1135 or 1144-1146; RC 15; Pref. P 1, p. 699

OR: Mass of Our Lord Jesus Christ, the Eternal High Priest (1st Thu.)
AP 1348-1349; RC 15; Pref. P 1, p. 699

5. Fri. Friday of the 1st Week of Advent
ALL 18; Pref. P 1, p. 699

OR: Mass of the Most Sacred Heart of Jesus (1st Fri.)
AP 1352-1354; RC 18; Pref. P 45, p. 1353

6. Sat. Saturday of the 1st Week of Advent
ALL 21; Pref. P 1, p. 699

OR: St. Nicholas, B (950)
AP 1128-1131; RC 21; Pref. P 1, p. 699

OR: Mass of the Immaculate Heart of the BVM (1st Sat.)
AP 1069-1071; RC 21; Pref. P 56-57, pp. 715-716

7. **Sun. SECOND SUNDAY OF ADVENT**
ALL **672**; Creed; Pref. P 1, p. **82**

8. **Mon. THE IMMACULATE CONCEPTION OF THE BLESSED VIRGIN MARY (Sol) (Holyday of Obligation)**
ALL **1497**; Gloria, Creed; Pref. P 58, p. **1502**

9. Tue. Tuesday of the 2nd Week in Advent
ALL 29; Pref. P 1, p. 699

OR: St. Juan Diego Cuauhtlatoatzin (952)
AP 1158-1160; RC 29; Pref. P. 1, p. 699

10. Wed. Wednesday of the 2nd Week in Advent
ALL 32; Pref. P 1, p. 699

11. Thu. Thursday of the 2nd Week in Advent
ALL 35; Pref. P 1, p. 699

OR: St. Damasus I, Po (953)
AP 1125-1128; RC 36; Pref. P 1, p. 699

12. Fri. OUR LADY OF GUADALUPE (F) (954)
AP 954-955; RC 1187-1208; Pref. P 56-57, pp. 715-716

13. Sat. St. Lucy, V & M (Mem) (955)
AP 1122-1123 or 1148-1152; RC 43; Pref. P 1, p. 699

14. **Sun. THIRD SUNDAY OF ADVENT**
ALL **678**; Creed; Pref. P 1, p. **82**

15. Mon. Monday of the 3rd Week of Advent
ALL 45; Pref. P 1, p. 699

16. Tue. Tuesday of the 3rd Week of Advent
ALL 48; Pref. P 1, p. 699

17. Wed. Wednesday of the 3rd Week of Advent
ALL 63; Pref. P 2, p. 699

18. Thu. Thursday of the 3rd Week of Advent
ALL 66; Pref. P 2, p. 699

19. Fri. Friday of the 3rd Week of Advent
ALL 70; Pref. P 2, p. 699

20. Sat. Saturday of the 3rd Week of Advent
ALL 74; Pref. P 2, p. 699

21. **Sun. FOURTH SUNDAY OF ADVENT**
ALL **684**; Creed; Pref. P 2, p. **82**

22. Mon. Monday of the 4th Week of Advent
ALL 81, Prof. P 2, p 699

23. Tue. Tuesday of the 4th Week of Advent
ALL 84; (Opt. Or. of St. John of Kanty, Pr, p. 958)
Pref. P 2, p. 699

24. Wed. Wednesday of the 4th Week of Advent
ALL 88; Pref. P 2, p. 699

EVENING: **VIGIL MASS OF THE NATIVITY OF THE LORD [CHRISTMAS] (Sol)**
ALL **139**; Gloria, Creed; Pref. P 3-5, pp. **83-84**

25. **Thu. NATIVITY OF THE LORD CHRISTMAS (Sol)**
NIGHT: ALL **146**; Gloria, Creed; Pref. P 3-5, pp. **83-84**
DAWN: ALL **151**; Gloria, Creed; Pref. P 3-5, pp. **83-84**
DAY: ALL **156**; Gloria, Creed; Pref. P 3-5, pp. **83-84**

26. Fri. ST. STEPHEN, THE FIRST MARTYR (F)
ALL 93; Pref. P 3-5, pp. 700-701

27. Sat. ST. JOHN, APOSTLE & EVANGELIST (F)
ALL 96; Gloria; Pref. P 3-5, pp. 700-701

28. **Sun. THE HOLY FAMILY OF JESUS, MARY, & JOSEPH (F)**
ALL **691**; Gloria, Creed; Pref. P 3-5, pp. **83-84**

29. Mon. 5th Day in the Octave of the Nativity of the Lord [Christmas]
ALL 103; Gloria; (Opt. Or. St. Thomas Becket, B & M, p. 959)
Pref. P 3-5, pp. 700-701

30. Tue. 6th Day in the Octave of the Nativity of the Lord [Christmas]
ALL 106; Gloria; Pref. P 3-5, pp. 700-701

31. Wed. 7th Day in the Octave of the Nativity of the Lord [Christmas]
ALL 109; Gloria; (Opt. Or. St. Sylvester I, Po, p. 959)
Pref. P 3-5, pp. 700-701

The Mass Explained

Revised and Expanded Edition

By Msgr. James P. Moroney

In a three-pronged approach, this book explores the theological meaning of the Mass, examines the role to which baptized Catholics are called in its celebration, and helps readers to discover the meaning of its words, songs, gestures, and ritual actions. Illustrated. 176 pages. Size 5 x 7. Flexible full-color paper cover.

No. 104/04

ISBN: 978-0-89942-104-9

Price: $8.95

OTHER OUTSTANDING CATHOLIC BOOKS

TREASURY OF NOVENAS—By Rev. Lawrence Lovasik, S.V.D. More than forty popular Novenas carefully arranged for private prayer in accord with the Liturgical Year on the Feasts of Jesus, Mary, and Favorite Saints. With color illustrations. **No. 345**

DAILY REFLECTIONS WITH MARY—By Rev. Rawley Myers. A beautifully illustrated and printed book that gives thirty-one prayerful Marian reflections plus a large selection of prayers to Our Lady. Every page is written out of deep love for Mary and inculcates a great devotion to her. **No. 372**

THE IMITATION OF CHRIST—By Thomas à Kempis. The one book that is second only to the Bible in popularity. Large type. Illustrated. **No. 320**

THE IMITATION OF MARY—By Rev. A. de Rouville, S.J. Companion volume to **The Imitation of Christ.** Large type. Illustrated. **No. 330**

LIVES OF THE SAINTS—Short life of a Saint and prayer for every day of the year. Over 50 illustrations. Ideal for daily meditation and private study. **No. 870**

PRAYERS FOR ALL OCCASIONS—By Rev. Francis Evans. Inspiring prayer book with a wealth of timely prayers for any occasion. With large type and printed in two colors. **No. 917**

PRAYERS FOR URGENT OCCASIONS—By Bernard Marie, O.F.S. Beautiful prayer book containing the prayers and devotions that will be of help in times of trial. Printed in two colors. **No. 918**

FAVORITE PRAYERS TO OUR LADY—By A. M. Buono. Contains prayers to Mary under her titles, for novenas and devotions, for various occasions, for liturgical times, and for every month and each day of the week. Printed in two colors. **No. 919**

CATHOLIC TREASURY OF PRAYERS—A prayer companion for all time. Features sections devoted to the Mass, the Psalms, and prayers to Our Blessed Mother, St. Joseph, and Patron Saints. 176 pages. **No. 938**

OTHER OUTSTANDING CATHOLIC BOOKS

KNOW . . . LOVE . . . and LIVE
the Mass with a
"Saint Joseph Missal"

Guide is No. 920/G
978-1-937913-91-5